D1505562

14 Tests
All Leaders
Must Face

*Understanding the
Seasons of Refinement*

LIFE IMPACT SERIES

FRANK DAMAZIO

CITYCHRISTIAN
PUBLISHING
WWW.CITYCHRISTIANPUBLISHING.COM

PUBLISHED BY CITY CHRISTIAN PUBLISHING

9200 NE Fremont, Portland, Oregon 97220

City Christian Publishing is a ministry of City Bible Church and is dedicated to serving the local church and its leaders through the production and distribution of quality equipping resources. It is our prayer that these materials, proven in the context of the local church, will equip leaders in exalting the Lord and extending His kingdom.

For a free catalog of additional resources from City Christian Publishing, please call 1-800-777-6057 or visit our web site at www.citychristianpublishing.com.

14 Tests All Leaders Must Face

ISBN: 1-59383-029-7

Cover design by DesignPoint, Inc.
Interior design and typeset by Katherine Lloyd, Bend, Oregon.

All Scripture quotations, unless otherwise indicated,
are taken from The King James Version of the Bible.
In some Scripture references, italics have been added by the author for emphasis.

First Edition, July 2005

Printed in the United States of America

TABLE OF CONTENTS

Chapter 1

RESPONDING
TO THE TESTING

When American Airlines trains its pilots, the company first seeks to prove its pilots' abilities with the use of a flight simulator. This device is designed to present the pilots with a variety of problematic situations so that they will be able to handle any emergency that they may face while in the air. The flight simulation test begins with simple problems and then builds up to catastrophic proportions. What's interesting is that the airlines never tests the pilots beyond their abilities but slowly gives them more difficult problems when they have mastered the previous ones. These mature pilots, upon completing their courses, are then fully prepared and ready to handle any problems that may come their way.

Does this scenario paint a picture in your mind of how God deals with all those whom He is preparing to do His work? Think about it. You can choose certain things in life: where you live, what you drive, what you eat, what clothes you wear, what kind of friends you have and so on. It's your choice! What you can't choose is whether you will face trials and tests. In God's economy, you have no choice in the matter. The tests God has chosen for you will come your way. You can count on that!

Modern man responds to difficulty by removing it. We are the epitome of an obstacle-defying society where mountains get bulldozed, bridges are built over rivers, and sickness is overcome with surgeries and prescriptions. But what happens when the obstacles don't move? Do we then develop our own spiritual justification based on taking Scripture out of context like, "I can remove all things in Christ?" We are so quick to devise sure-fire methods for the removal of all obstacles, inconveniences, trials, or pressures. When we do this, we tend to forget the reason why we are facing these life hurdles in the first place.

Don't forget: trials are a means or instrument of testing that reveals the true inner world and character of the individual. James 1:2 says this: "Consider it pure joy, my brothers, whenever you face trials of many kinds." Consider it pure joy? What?! Does this sound like the way you would truly respond to trials and tests? In this verse, we see that your response, which comes from the deepest part of your heart or character, is key to whether you will pass the test.

The "various" trials cited in James 1:2 are like a myriad of unexplainable bad circumstances that can fall upon any area of your life, whether physical, financial, social, or spiritual. The Greek word for "trials" found in this verse is *peinasmois*, which means to try something so as to know its worth, a proving through adversity, afflictions, or troubles. The testing is done with the purpose of discerning the quality of the object tested. It is the making of a person who will become a trusted servant, who will not break under pressure or throw in the towel when tried and discouraged.

First Thessalonians 3:3 also says, "no one should be shaken by these afflictions; for you yourselves know that we are appointed to this." It's clear from this verse that tests are assigned to us, appointed and on their way to encounter us. These trials and tests may involve some level of suffering that is deserved or undeserved, fair or unfair. This is because we are the sons and daughters of God as seen in Romans 8:17: "and if children, then heirs—heirs of God and joint heirs with Christ, if indeed we suffer with Him, that we may also be glorified together." And 1 Peter 4:19 confirms this: "Therefore let those who suffer according to the will of God commit their souls to Him in doing good, as to a faithful Creator."

Trials. Crises. Testings. Adversity. Contradictions.... How will you respond? What will be revealed in your character? Are you ready to do all that God has called you to do? The storms of life come in quietly and usually without warning. Imagine fishing on a beautiful, calm lake; within minutes, a torrential downpour comes out of nowhere, threatening your very life. When this happens, will you be ready?

Testings originate in the mind and will of God to expose our weaknesses and deliver us from those things that hide deep within our character that could harm or even destroy us. This is God's good purpose for our lives and is referenced by Moses in Deuteronomy 8:2: "And you shall remember that the LORD your God led you all the way these forty years in the wilderness, to humble you and test you, to know what was in your heart, whether you would keep His commandments or not."

Here are some Scriptures to ponder if you still doubt that tests will inevitably come your way:

DEUTERONOMY 13:3

"You shall not listen to the words of that prophet or that dreamer of dreams, for the LORD your God is testing you to know whether you love the LORD your God with all your heart and with all your soul."

2 Chronicles 32:31

"However, regarding the ambassadors of the princes of Babylon, whom they sent to him to inquire about the wonder that was done in the land, God withdrew from him, in order to test him, that He might know all that was in his heart."

Psalm 7:9

"Oh, let the wickedness of the wicked come to an end, but establish the just; for the righteous God tests the hearts and minds."

Psalm 11:5

"The LORD tests the righteous, but the wicked and the one who loves violence His soul hates."

PSALM 17:3

"You have tested my heart; You have visited me in the night; You have tried me and have found nothing; I have purposed that my mouth shall not transgress."

MATTHEW 4:4

"But He answered and said, 'It is written, "Man shall not live by bread alone, but by every word that proceeds from the mouth of God."'"

1 PETER 4:12

"Beloved, do not think it strange concerning the fiery trial which is to try you, as though some strange thing happened to you."

MATTHEW 7:24-27

"Therefore whoever hears these sayings of Mine, and does them, I will liken him to a wise man who built his house on the rock: and the rain descended, the floods came, and the winds blew and beat on that house; and it did not fall, for it was founded on the rock. But everyone who hears these sayings of Mine, and does not do them, will be like a foolish man who built his house on the sand: and the rain descended, the floods came, and the winds blew and beat on that house; and it fell. And great was its fall."

1 Corinthians 3:12-15

"Now if anyone builds on this foundation with gold, silver, precious stones, wood, hay, straw, each one's work will become clear; for the Day will declare it, because it will be revealed by fire; and the fire will test each one's work, of what sort it is. If anyone's work which he has built on it endures, he will receive a reward. If anyone's work is burned, he will suffer loss; but he himself will be saved, yet so as through fire."

1 Peter 1:6-8

"In this you greatly rejoice, though now for a little while, if need be, you have been grieved by various trials, that the genuineness of your faith, being much more precious than gold that perishes, though it is tested by fire, may be found to praise, honor, and glory at the revelation of Jesus Christ, whom having not seen you love. Though now you do not see Him, yet believing, you rejoice with joy inexpressible and full of glory."

You should know by now that you are destined for trials. The good news is that you are not alone.

Trials and tests are encountered by all: the small and the great, the new believer and the mature believer, rich and poor alike. All are afflicted, with no exceptions.

In Genesis 45:7-8, we read: "And God sent me before you to preserve a posterity for you in the earth, and to save your lives by a great deliverance. So now it was not you who sent me here, but God; and He has made me a father to Pharaoh, and lord of all his house, and a ruler throughout all the land of Egypt." If we can grasp this same attitude that Joseph displayed, we will greatly profit from all the tests of life that were either allowed by or sent from God. We can respond with faith and assurance because we belong to God. We are God's possession. God is in control at all times. No trial or test reaches us apart from God's explicit decree and specific permission. This is confirmed in Acts 14:22, "Strengthening the souls of the disciples, exhorting them to continue in the faith and saying, 'We must through many tribulations enter the kingdom of God.'" And Acts 9:16, "For I will show him how many things he must suffer for My name's sake."

God may not initiate all our trials, but by the time they reach us, they are in God's hand to use for our good. When life, other people, or just plain accidents bring us sorrow, we can answer like Joseph did. He forgave his brothers for selling him into slavery when he was a young man and said in Genesis 50:20, "As for you, you meant evil against me, but God meant it for good."

God has a "load limit" for our tests and trials. Diesel trucks that travel the highways of our nation are subjected to a "load limit." This means that there is a limit as to how much weight trucks can haul to their destinations. If the trucks exceed the proposed weight limit, then the roads will eventually fall apart because they are not designed to support such heavy vehicles. Likewise, God knows how much testing we can bear. He has a definite "load limit" assigned to each of us during our times of stretching.

The custom-made test God brings into our lives is like a blazing torch for God to see into the depth of our being. In this state of vulnerability, we may see many things about ourselves that we little expected to see. We may find our faith weak when we thought it was strong or our vision dim when we thought it was bright and clear. True tests cause us to reassess life's real values as we take time to carefully evaluate what is important. In this process, what is false can be stripped away and the genuine part that continues to trust God will develop victorious, positive endurance. Testing clears the mind, removes the superficial, and exposes the temporal and wrong views of life

(1 Peter 1:23-25, Revelations 2:9, Isaiah 40:6-8). The Scriptures clearly teach us that tests come to try the genuineness of our faith, to discover the latent corruption of our hearts, to purify and sanctify our motivations, to call into existence the grace of the Holy Spirit, and to cultivate a deeper understanding of God's ways and character. A clay pot sitting in the sun will always be a clay pot. It has to go through the white heat of the furnace in order to become porcelain.

I have laid out 14 tests that all leaders must face at different times in life and at varying intensities. These will help any and all "to be" leaders to prepare for what God may do in their character-building journey. Are you ready to be tested?

Chapter 2

THE TIME TEST

Definition—In the Time Test, by all outward appearances, God does not seem to be fulfilling the word He gave a leader in the past. The Time Test tries a leader's patience, forcing him* to trust God to fulfill his call and ministry in His own time and way.

Purpose—This test gives the leader an opportunity to grow in faith. Every leader has a measure of

---

*Unless otherwise stated, whenever the masculine gender is used, both men and women are included.

trust and confidence in God. Because each must lead people to believe in God for every detail of life, however, a leader must be given more faith with which to strengthen his own people. The Time Test also purifies a leader's motives and attitudes. During times of delay, a leader can see how his own impure, selfish, or proud motives and attitudes can cloud his desires before the Lord. God desires transparent motives and attitudes in each of His leaders.

In the Time Test, God proves Himself to be a miracle-working, faithful God to everyone He has called to the service of His kingdom. Many times, a leader believes that his own activity and striving can fulfill God's vision for His Church. Though God's leaders must cooperate with God's plan, God always delights in using the weaknesses of men to give Him all of the glory (1 Corinthians 1:26-31). During the Time Test, when men's plans can only fail, God arranges a miracle to bring all of the glory to Himself. As He does the miracle, He demonstrates His faithfulness to His leaders.

Biblical Illustration—Abraham: The story of the patriarch Abraham shows the Time Test at work. Abraham was 75 years old when God called him out of Haran to travel to Canaan (Genesis 12:1-9). God promised Abraham he'd possess all of Canaan from the Euphrates south. Being childless, the patriarch had made his home-born slave, Eleazar, to be his heir. But God promised Abraham that he would have a child of his own as heir (15:4). Abraham did not wait through God's Time Test. At the age of 86, he had a son, Ishmael, through his concubine Hagar (16:1-4). Not until Abraham was 100 did God bring His promise to pass in Abraham's son Isaac (17:1 and 18:10). Abraham had to wait 25 years before he received God's promise of a natural son for his heir.

Many leaders today complain if they must wait five or seven years before seeing God's will fulfilled. With Abraham, they say, "Oh, that Ishmael might live before Thee!" (Genesis 17:18). Instead, they must submit to God's Time Test and, with patient endurance, allow it to work faith and purity into their lives.

Chapter 3

THE WORD TEST

Definition—In the Word Test, the leader experiences circumstances that seem to nullify the written or living Word of God. "How can the known will of God possibly come to pass in my life?" is the leader's cry during this time. Many feel that because they have been filled and called by God's Spirit, they should never experience darkness or confusion as long as they do not fall into sin.

But the Word Test is no accident. In fact, God purposely allows contrary situations in a leader's life and ministry. No leader is exempt from these times of trial and misunderstanding. During the Word Test, God has not forgotten or contradicted His promise. But He desires to accomplish certain purposes that are as yet totally unknown to the leader. If the leader endures with patience, trust, and obedience, he will eventually find himself rejoicing in the Lord's wisdom and skill in the planning and use of these seemingly antagonistic experiences.

Purpose—God uses the Word Test to cause a leader to reject his own resources and depend solely on God's strength to bring God's Word to pass. This is a difficult task for a leader, especially for a man of many strengths and abilities. A talented leader can easily trust more in himself than in God.

The Word Test also extends the reach of the kingdom of heaven. A leader may plan to reach a certain number of people with the gospel. But through the Word Test, encouragingly, he will discover that God reached more people after His Word became more than just an untested promise. The trial of God's Word gives a leader further testimony of God's power and faithfulness, to share with more people.

Biblical Illustration—Joseph (Genesis 37-45): Joseph was the eleventh son of Jacob, the first by his wife Rachel (Genesis 30:24), and Jacob's favorite son (37:3). At the age of 17, Joseph received a word from the Lord in the form of two dreams. In one, his family's sheaves bowed down to his sheave in the field. In the other, the sun, moon, and eleven stars bowed down to him (37:5-11). Since the two dreams represented his eventual authority over his parents and brothers, he became an object of jealousy. Joseph's brothers sold him to an Ishmaelite caravan from Gilead that was traveling down into Egypt (37:25-28). There, he was sold to Potiphar, Pharaoh's officer (37:29-36).

Joseph was falsely accused of trying to seduce Potiphar's wife, and was banished to prison (39:7-23). There, one of his last hopes of ever getting a word of reminder to the king about his imprisonment were dashed when the king's chief cupbearer did not remember to tell the king about Joseph after he himself was released from prison (40:23).

Through all of these contradictory circumstances, God's Word to Joseph was tested. How could he rule over his brethren as an Egyptian slave? How could Joseph rule from a prison cell?

The Psalmist very accurately describes what happened to Joseph and his promise from God. *"(God) sent a man before them, Joseph, who was sold as a slave. They afflicted his feet with fetters; he himself was laid in irons. Until the time that his word came to pass, the word of the Lord tested* (refined) *him"* Psalm 105:17-19.

Joseph waited approximately fourteen years to

see the fulfillment of God's word to him. With great patience, Joseph waited in prison until God brought him out through a command of the king (Psalm 105:20, 21). During Joseph's experience of the Word Test, God developed character, wisdom, and humility in his life.

All leaders must likewise see the instructions of the hand of the Lord during God's Word Test in their lives and ministries.

Chapter 4

THE CHARACTER TEST

Definition—In the Character Test, the leader is surrounded by ungodliness that attempts to pull him in its direction. The leader may be tempted to sin in the lust of the flesh, the lust of the eyes, or the pride of life. In order to develop leaders with strong, godly character qualities—love, joy, peace, patience, kindness, self-control, faithfulness—God puts leaders in fiery places so they may learn to stand strong in Him.

Purpose—The Character Test shows to the leader the areas of weakness in his own personality. When God brings a situation into a leader's life which requires much patience, he realizes he must call on more of God's grace. An area of need usually surfaces, where he must allow God to work. Every leader has hidden character deficiencies of which he is totally unaware, until confronted with a specific situation that demands a godly response. To expose his own true inward self to every leader, God uses the Character Test.

The Character Test also motivates a leader to stand up boldly against the powers of darkness around him. Too many leaders are shy about proclaiming the truth. Too many wait until they are attacked from the outside before they take the initiative of preaching the gospel. Many need to be confronted with evil so they will stand up boldly for the name of the Lord and His righteousness.

Biblical Illustration—Samuel (1 Samuel 2-3):
Samuel was the son of a religious Ephraimite, Elkanah, and his wife Hannah. Samuel is regarded as the last and greatest of the judges and the first of the prophets (Acts 13:20 and 3:24). Samuel, however, was born into a corrupt situation.

Eli, the high priest at this time, had grown physically and spiritually dull, and the light in the tabernacle had almost extinguished (1 Samuel 2:27-36 and 3:1-3). Eli was a corrupt high priest who did not discipline his sons, Hophni and Phinehas, who committed fornication with women at the very door of the tabernacle of the congregation. Because of this morally corrupt situation, God overthrew Eli's succession and introduced Samuel as the leader of Israel's spiritual and secular affairs.

Though a very young boy in the midst of a corrupt priesthood, Samuel worshipped God and kept himself from sin. The young prophet could have fallen into sin like Eli's sons, but he chose not to. Samuel's story demonstrates that leaders do not have to be corrupted by their environments. Samuel kept himself pure in the midst of sin and immorality. He underwent God's Character Test and remained righteous.

Chapter 5

THE MOTIVATION TEST

Definition—This is a heavenly "examination" in which God exposes to the leader what inner and outer forces influence his decision-making processes. God will arrange situations to reveal a leader's true inner intentions, thoughts, values, and priorities that cause him to make choices or act in a certain way.

A leader may not always know why he does something. What appears to motivate him, from an outer inspection, may be a far cry from internal motives.

Purpose—God uses the Motivation Test to disclose those inner drives and to purify them into desires for the glory of God, the salvation of souls, and the edification of the Church. A leader may serve God for what he can get out of God, rather than what he can give to Him or His people. A person may use his gifts to glorify himself, rather than God. God puts His leaders through Motivation Tests to expose unrighteous drives, and then to replace them with motives of His Spirit, and true love out of a pure heart.

Biblical Illustration—Balaam (Numbers 22-24): The story of Balaam, the prophet, shows the Motivation Tests at work. Balak, the son of Zippor and the king of Moab, had seen how Israel had defeated all of her enemies in the land. He feared they would destroy his nation as well.

Consequently, he offered to pay the prophet Balaam to curse the Israelites to put an end to their victories (22:7). Balaam responded to Balak that the Lord had told him not to go with the elders of Moab to curse the people of Israel.

Balak tried again, sending more numerous and distinguished ambassadors to persuade Balaam otherwise (22:15). This time, the Lord told Balaam to go with the elders of Moab and Midian, but to speak only the word the Lord gave him to speak (22:20). Balaam did go to Balak, but each time he inquired of the Lord, the Lord told him to bless Israel.

Needless to say, this greatly upset the Moabites and Midianites! Through it all, God was testing Balaam's motivation. Would he sell out, or would he be faithful to God's word? God allowed Balak to tempt the prophet's motivation continually, and every time, the size of the bribe grew (22:7, 15, 17). Unfortunately, it appears that Balaam's motivation did not stay pure, though he initially tried to remain faithful to speaking only the word of the Lord (23:12, 26). Balaam failed this Motivation Test from the Lord (2 Peter 2:15; Jude 11; Revelation 2:14), who allowed him to be tempted with much money if he would only disobey God and curse God's people.

God will test and try a leader to know what is in his heart. He desires to use pure leaders, whose motivation for ministry is the glory of God and the salvation of souls.

Chapter 6

THE SERVANT TEST

Definition—In the Servant Test, a man is asked to do menial tasks that seem below his high calling in God. No menial task is below any true servant of God. But especially before (or even during) his time of fully giving himself to prayer and the Word instead of "waiting on tables" (see Acts 6:2-4), God tests a leader to see if he is willing to do menial service.

Purpose—The Servant Test reveals whether a ministry's motivation is simply to be in the public eye and receive service, or if he truly desires to help and serve. Those in authority over that ministry (remember that we use the word "ministry" to refer to a person who ministers) will see how well he passes the test. God may instruct authorities over a ministry to use this test to discern the person's commitment to service. Does a young man think it below his ministry to sweep the church floor? Does a young woman believe it is beneath her calling to sing in a large choir and not to solo? These are revealing questions.

This test also reveals to God's governmental ministries what it feels like to do different jobs in the local church. How many pastors today cannot appreciate the effort and time a church janitor puts in, unless they experience some of it themselves? How can a man expect to communicate to an adult-level class unless he also relates to college-level groups? Every leader needs personal experience in different jobs in the Church, so he can better understand and communicate with people in those positions when he acts as, for example, a church pastor.

Biblical Illustration—Elisha (1 Kings 19): Elisha is a pointed example of the Servant Test. When Elijah found Elisha, who was to become his prophetical heir, Elisha was plowing in the field with twelve yoke of oxen before him. This probably means that Elisha was plowing at the end of eleven other men, each driving a plow and pair of oxen. This was probably a humbling position—following eleven other pairs of oxen would certainly not lend itself to a sweet fragrance, cleanliness, or fresh air. The dust of the field was, without a doubt, thick in the air. Was this the proper place for a future prophet of Israel, who was going to do more miracles than his predecessor?

1 Kings 19:21 states that after Elisha burned

his farming equipment, *"he arose and followed Elijah and ministered to him."* Elisha became the servant of Elijah, though he would succeed him. 2 Kings 3:11 states, *"Elisha, the son of Shaphat, is here, who used to pour water on the hands of Elijah,"* confirming that his larger ministry began with "menial" service. Ministry is not the end of servanthood, either. It only means that a leader now must serve even more people in an even greater capacity.

Chapter 7

THE WILDERNESS TEST

Definition—In the Wilderness Test, God directly or indirectly guides a leader (or future leader) into a materially and/or spiritually dry and desolate place. When no fruit comes from his life or ministry, a leader feels he is in this test. In such times, a leader wonders whether he really received a call of God upon his life, because he appears to have no direct involvement in the true, living work of the kingdom of God. Sometimes, a leader is left with no one else to talk to but God himself.

Purpose—The Wilderness Test increases a leader's appreciation for the good things that God has already put in his life.

This test also teaches the leader how to discern whether the Lord alone sustains his spiritual life, or if he draws from his ministry activity to sustain his relationship with God. Does a leader's prayer, Word, and evangelism activities drop off just because he is not in "full-time" Christian work and supported by a local church? If so, his activities may be sustaining his walk with God, rather than his own personal relationship with God.

God also uses the Wilderness Test to strip the leader of all the wisdom and ways of the world, and to teach him the ways of His Spirit. Every leader must learn that God's ways are different from his own. Sometimes, the best way to learn this is through dry and lonely desert experiences.

A wasteland experience also drives a leader to

cultivate his life in prayer and the Word. Many leaders need dry places to exhaust the reservoir of sheer nervous energy that they draw from to serve the Lord. God desires His leaders not to strive for Him in fearful, nervous energy, but to walk with Him in restful, spiritual peace. The Wilderness Test motivates a leader to seek the Lord in a consistent life of prayer and the Word, to find the genuine and most fruitful source of strength—God Himself.

Biblical Illustration—Moses (Exodus 2, 3): Moses stands out as an appropriate example of the Wilderness Test. Moses learned that his killing of an Egyptian, who was beating an Israelite (Exodus 2:11), was known to Pharaoh and the palace. He fled across the border to Midian for safety (2:15). There he married Zipporah, daughter of the Midianite shepherd-priest Jethro, and she bore him two sons.

Acts 7:29,30 states that forty years passed before an angel of the Lord called Moses to deliver God's people Israel from Egyptian slavery (Exodus 3:1). Why was this great man of God kept in the wilderness forty years, shepherding sheep, before God called him to his great ministry as Israel's deliverer and lawgiver? One belief: God took forty years to strip Moses of all his Egyptian learning and prepare him for his work (Acts 7:22). Only then could Moses truly learn God's ways, the only means by which God could lead His chosen people out of the land of bondage.

It is highly unlikely that Moses learned how to hear the voice of God, or to use the rod of God to do miracles, while he was in Egypt. In Egypt he had most probably learned hieroglyphic and hieratic scripts, the reproduction of texts, letter-writing, archery and other "civilized" arts. But he probably did not learn much about the ways of God's Spirit.

In forty years in the desert, Moses learned what he needed to know to lead God's people out of Egypt.

Today, some leaders complain much about the far fewer years that God uses a seeming wasteland to teach them valuable spiritual truths. May every leader consider every wilderness test a special class in the school of God's Spirit, from which he can derive much spiritual benefit.

Chapter 8

THE MISUNDER-STANDING TEST

Definition—The Misunderstanding Test occurs when those hearing a leader do not receive (or reject) the correct meaning he is trying to communicate. People may misinterpret or mistake the true significance of his actions, words, attitudes or motives.

Purpose—The Misunderstanding Test causes a leader to look for new or better ways of bringing across his feelings. It also causes him to examine his basic attitudes and motivations in communication. Many times, people will misunderstand what a person is trying to say just because the communicator has an attitude that is too hard, harsh, or angry when he tries to say it.

When a leader discovers major misunderstandings, he is motivated to trust totally in God, and not in his own skills as a communicator. In the New Testament, God was the one who opened the hearts of different people to believe the gospel message. A leader must trust the ministry of the Holy Spirit to quicken the truth of what he is communicating. God desires every leader to trust that His Word, through the Holy Spirit, will accomplish the task of building His kingdom.

The Misunderstanding Test is especially humbling to leaders because it involves those who are very dear and close to the leader.

To be free mentally, emotionally, and spiritually,

a leader must make room in his heart for some misunderstanding. Anyone who preaches the Word of God will be misinterpreted at one time or another. The key for every leader in this is to keep his heart free from anger and resentment, and to allow the Lord Jesus to turn the situation into good. Through prayer and trust in God, every leader will learn many lessons of wisdom from times of misunderstanding.

Biblical Illustration—the Lord Jesus Christ: A biblical term for misunderstanding is the word "contradiction." Hebrews 12:3 states this about Jesus: *"For consider him who has endured such hostility* (KJV "contradiction") *by sinners against himself, so that you may not grow weary and lose heart."* Jesus is the prime example of the test of intentional and unintentional misunderstanding. He suffered this not only from the Jewish people in general, but especially by the Jewish religious rulers, and even by His close followers.

When Jesus said, *"Eat my flesh and drink my blood"* (John 6:60), some of His close disciples misunderstood and left Him. Being forsaken by outsiders is one thing, but rejections by one's own disciples over a misunderstanding is another thing. And most of Jesus' own people, the Jews, rejected Him because they did not correctly understand how He fulfilled Bible prophecy.

Chapter 9

THE PATIENCE TEST

Definition—The Patience Test happens when a leader's expectations in God are not fulfilled "on schedule." Patience is one of the fruits of the Holy Spirit (Galatians 5:22). This word comes from a Latin word which means "to suffer." In the Patience Test, God challenges a leader to wait patiently, or to endure some tribulation, without complaint. To grow in patience, a leader must bear pain or trouble without losing self-control or becoming a disturbance to others. In portraying this quality, a leader calmly tolerates delay while refusing to be provoked by it.

Purpose—To pass the Patience Test, a leader must have yielded his rights to Jesus Christ already, so that he is able to wait for Him to return his expectations to him in His own timing, and as undeserved blessings. Every leader has certain expectations, not only in his own life and ministry, but also of others. In not attempting to "play God" in his own life or in the lives of others, a humble leader will yield to the Lord even some very good and appropriate goals. The leader knows that God will use a delay of fulfillment to accomplish what He desires. A leader must yield rights to the Lord constantly. The Lord will motivate him to do this by using the demands of other people in the Patience Test.

Biblical Illustration—Noah (Genesis 5-7): Like the other early patriarchs, Noah was given a great many years to live. He was 500 years old when his wife bore their first son (Genesis 5:32), and 600 years old at the time of the Flood (7:11). Noah was probably 480 years old when God informed him of His plan to destroy the earth with water (6:3, 1 Peter 3:20). It was for some 120 years, then, that he preached repentance to his generation, but to no avail. God allowed a period of 120 years of grace in which Noah was to build an ark for his family and the animals (6:13-22), and preach to his generation about God's coming judgment.

During the entire 120 years of his preaching, Noah saw no one repent of his sins and turn to God for mercy. One hundred twenty years is a long time for any preacher to continue to preach without results. This long endurance required much patience from Noah. He kept preaching and preaching, but without conversions. It was only because God gave divine grace and patience to

Noah that he could endure this test so well. At the end of his Patience Test, only he and his family found themselves safely in the ark that they had built. The scoffers perished in the flood waters outside. Noah's patience paid off for him and his family in the end. Patience will pay off for every leader who calmly leaves the results and details of his ministry in the capable hand of the Lord.

Chapter 10

THE FRUSTRATION TEST

Definition—A leader undergoes the Frustration Test when he feels that his life or ministry goals cannot be achieved. People or circumstances may prevent him from gratifying his conscious or unconscious desires and goals. A ministry especially experiences this feeling when he finds no logical or rational reason why his efforts are being baffled, foiled, or confused.

Purpose—The Frustration Test causes a leader to re-examine his spiritual priorities. Is he giving enough time to prayer and the Word? Is he giving enough attention to his wife and family? God will many times bring frustration to a leader's life and ministry when his priorities need re-adjustment.

Frustration also causes the leader to put more fervor into his primary spiritual battle against opposition to the simple gospel of Jesus Christ. With his other goals and activities temporarily out of gear, a leader may realize that he has neglected the simple preaching of the Good News to the lost. With that spiritual priority adjusted, God will release him from the test of frustration.

Biblical Illustration—Paul (2 Corinthians 11): A definite sense of frustration comes through these words from the apostle Paul:

2 CORINTHIANS 11:17 – 12:1

"That which I speak, I speak it not after the Lord, but as it were foolishly, in this confidence of boasting. Seeing that many glory after the flesh, I will glory also. For ye suffer fools gladly, seeing ye yourselves are wise. For ye suffer, if a man brings you into bondage, if a man devour you, if a man take of you, if a man exalt himself, if a man smite you on the face. I speak as concerning reproach, as though we had been weak. Howbeit wherinsoever any is bold, (I speak foolishly,) I am bold also. Are they Hebrews? So am I. Are they Israelites? So am I. Are they seed of Abraham? So am I. Are they ministers of Christ? (I speak as a fool) I am more; in labours more abundant, in stripes above measure, in prisons more frequent, in deaths oft. Of the Jews five times received I (the) forty stripes save one. Thrice was I stoned, thrice I suffered shipwreck, a night and a day I have been in the deep; In journeyings often, in perils of waters, in perils of robbers, in perils by mine own countrymen, in perils by the heathen, in perils in the city, in perils in the wilderness, in perils in the sea, in perils among false brethren; In weariness and painfulness, in watchings often, in hunger and thirst, in fastings often, in cold and nakedness. Beside those things that are without, that which cometh upon me daily, the care of all the churches. Who is weak, and I am not weak? Who is offended, and I burn not? If I must needs glory, I will glory of the things which concern mine infirmities. The God and Father of our Lord Jesus Christ, which is blessed for evermore, knoweth that I lie not. In Damascus the governor under Aretas the king kept the city of the Damascenes with a garrison, desirous to apprehend me: And through a window in a basket was I let down by the wall, and escaped his hands. It is not expedient for me doubtless to glory. I will come to visions and revelations of the Lord."

We can sense Paul's frustration, especially in verse 28 and 29, where he says, "Beside those things that are without, that which cometh upon me daily, the care of all the churches. Who is weak and I am not weak? Who is offended, and I burn not?" Paul was a human being like every leader, and he had his times of bafflement and frustration, too. His answer to frustration, however, was a simple trust in the power of the Spirit over the natural. He declared by faith in the midst of frustration:

2 CORINTHIANS 4:8-17
"We are troubled on every side, yet not distressed; we are perplexed, but not in despair;

persecuted, but not forsaken; cast down, but not destroyed; always bearing about in the body the dying of the Lord Jesus, that the life also of Jesus might be made manifest in our body. For we which live are always delivered unto death for Jesus' sake, that the life also of Jesus might be made manifest in our mortal flesh. So then death worketh in us, but life in you. We having the same spirit of faith, according as it is written, I believed, and therefore have I spoken; we also believe, and therefore speak; knowing that he which raised up the Lord Jesus shall raise up us also by Jesus, and shall present us with you. For all things are for your sakes, that the abundant grace might through the thanksgiving of many redound to the glory of God. For which cause we faint not; but though our outward man perish, yet the inward man is renewed day by day. For our light affliction, which is but for a moment, worketh for us a far more exceeding and eternal weight of glory; while we look not at the things which are seen, but at the things which are not seen: for the things which are seen are temporal; but the things which are not seen are eternal."

Chapter 11

THE DISCOURAGEMENT TEST

Definition—A leader is going through the Discouragement Test when he allows circumstances or people to dishearten him and deprive him of courage in the Lord. A discouraged leader is deterred from an undertaking which he believed was God's will. During such times, a minister may lose his confidence or hope in

God, His provision, His promises, or His calling.

Purpose—Discouragement causes the leader to go to God in prayer, especially through the Psalms. The Psalms express most of the different conditions of heart that people face during their lifetime. The moods of the Psalms vary from joy over the defeat of one's enemies to the sorrow and depths of despair and discouragement. During the Discouragement Test, a leader should try to find the Psalm(s) that best express the mood of his soul, and then pray through it to God sincerely.

Discouraging times of stress and trial are not wrong. But the attitude one takes toward such circumstances can be, if one persists in self-pity or feelings of discouragement. A leader must learn through these times that his joy comes from delighting himself in the Lord, not delighting only in happy circumstances or positive responses from people. No leader will sustain his ministry without learning how to derive total joy and peace directly from God Himself.

The Discouragement Test also reveals the hidden, bad attitudes in a leader. Many leaders can rejoice in the Lord when everything is going the way they think things should. But how many allow themselves to complain and murmur when things go unexpectedly the other way? During discouragement, the Lord allows the leader to uncover poor attitudes in himself, for which he must ask God's forgiveness. A leader would be far better if God had never revealed these bad attitudes, than if he came to know them but still failed to repent of them. The spiritual principle here: we become responsible to do what God has showed us to do, and failure to obey both judges and condemns us.

Biblical Illustration—Elijah (1 Kings 19): Elijah became very discouraged when he learned that Israel had forsaken the Lord, and that queen Jezebel planned to kill him (10:2,3). In discouragement, Elijah fled from Jezebel. He left his servant in Beersheba, went a day's journey into the wilderness, sat under a juniper tree, and asked God to take his life (v. 4).

God's response included this statement: *"I have kept for myself seven thousand men who have not bowed the knee to Baal"* (see also Romans 11:4). And God also asked Elijah, *"What are you doing here?"* (vs. 9,13) when the prophet complained that he was the only one who had zeal for the Lord of hosts (vs. 10,14). Many times discouragement comes to a leader when he feels that he is the only one who is totally working for God. This can be alleviated, however, by developing a church along the patterns of God's

New Testament gifts and ministries. The congregation can have plurality of eldership, and members of the congregation can be taught how to find and function in their God-assigned spiritual gifts and ministries.

It is valuable to note what God spoke to Elijah during his time of discouragement, and to apply it to the leader today. (Study all of 1 Kings 19 to understand the context for the following comments.)

In response to Elijah's discouragement, the Lord told the prophet:

TO ELIJAH

"Arise, eat and drink." (vs.5, 6)

"Arise, eat and drink because the journey to Mount Horeb is too great for you." (vs.7,8)

"What are you doing here at a cave on Mount Horeb, Elijah?" (v.9)

"Go forth and stand on the mountain before the Lord. And behold the Lord was passing by!" (v.11)

"What are you doing here (at the entrance of the cave), *Elijah?"* (v.13)

"Go, return on your way to the wilderness of Damascus, and when you have arrived, you shall anoint Hazael king over Syria, and Jehu . . . you shall anoint king over Israel, and Elisha...you shall anoint as prophet in your place" (vs.15,16).

To apply this spiritual principle to Church leaders today:

TO THE LEADER

In discouragement, a leader's emotional energy is decreased. He may feel like lying down and sleeping just as Elijah did. The leader gains new strength as he arises and eats of the scroll of the Word of the Lord, and thereby also drinks of the Spirit of God. Standing and confessing the Word of God enables a leader to overcome discouragement.

During discouragement, God desires His leader to get away and seek His face in prayer. A leader is motivated to pray when he sees that, in himself, he has no strength to do God's will, but that in the Lord he does (as he eats the Word and drinks of the Spirit).

During discouragement, a leader is inclined to stop and lodge at a "mountaintop" place where he can hear the still, small voice of God. Every leader must learn how to press into the Lord during such times, until he receives a clear word from the Lord.

During this test, the Lord challenges His leaders to stand face-to-face with Him in their distress. A leader should not try to hide his discouragement from God, for He already knows of it.

During distress, even after knowing that the Lord will speak to him in a still, small voice, the leader is still tempted to run and hide from God. But the leader must not do so when he is discouraged. On the contrary, he must seek the Lord for a word concerning the next action that he should take, and then go do it.

When God speaks to the sincere and open leader who is discouraged, He will give him specific assignments. These activities help get a leader's mind off his own problems, and back onto doing the will of the Lord, and obeying His Word in everyday life.

Chapter 12

THE WARFARE TEST

Definition—The Warfare Test happens when a leader encounters violent spiritual opposition to his progress in the Spirit, or in his extending of God's kingdom. Though it happens in the realm of the spirit, it can find natural expression in conflicts with people, lack of response to one's ministry, or struggles of various sorts (including the feeling of unbearable temptation to sin).

Some people think that anointed leaders cannot be tempted like other people can. Recent leadership failures have proven that untrue! And the Bible says that even Jesus "was in all points tempted like we are, yet without sin" (Hebrews 4:15). The calling of God does not remove human susceptibility to temptation. Leaders must make a conscious effort to obey the Scripture, *walk in the Spirit and ye shall not fulfill the lusts of the flesh* (Galatians 5:16).

Purposes—Spiritual warfare forces the leader to grow stronger in the Spirit. In this, the spiritual realm is like the natural realm, where a muscle becomes stronger only through exercise and resistance. Hebrews 5:14 uses the word "exercise" when it states that solid spiritual food is for the mature, *who by reason of use have their senses exercised to discern booth good and evil.*

Some leaders are not mature because they do not train or exercise their spiritual senses enough. Through spiritual warfare, a leader learns how to use effectively his spiritual weapons of the Word, prayer, praise, and the name of the Lord Jesus Christ.

Biblical Illustration—Timothy (1 and 2 Timothy): Timothy was exhorted by the apostle Paul to give everything he could to succeeding in the tests of spiritual warfare. Due to his youth, the Greek nationality of his father, and the heresies of his day, Timothy was a natural target for spiritual attack. The following Scripture references indicate this spiritual fight:

1 TIMOTHY 1:18

"This command I entrust to you, Timothy, my son, in accordance with the prophecies previously made concerning you, that by them you might fight the good fight." .

1 TIMOTHY 4:7

"I have fought the good fight."

1 Timothy 6:12

"Fight the good fight of faith; take hold of the eternal life to which you were called."

2 Timothy 2:3,4

"Suffer hardship with me, as a good soldier of Christ Jesus. No soldier in active service entangles himself in the affairs of everyday life, so he may please the one who enlists him as a soldier."

Like Timothy, every leader must fight the good fight of faith. Just like the Christian life, the ministry is a battle to the last breath. Jesus Christ has won the battle for His people through His death and resurrection, but His victory must still be worked out into the full experience of the Church and the world.

The spiritual warfare of a pastor or teacher is to

preach the Word of God so powerfully that God's spiritual enemies in darkness will be defeated, and people converted to Jesus Christ. The battle consists also of the leader strongly holding on to his faith in Jesus Christ until the end. Satan tries every means of defeating the proclamation of the gospel and the growth of the Church. But try as he may, the spiritual victory belongs to every Christian leader as he uses the spiritual weapons that God has given him to win the battle.

Please remember that our spiritual warfare cannot be won with natural, carnal, worldly, human, or non-spiritual weapons. Throughout history, when the Church has trusted in human violence or unscriptural means of extending the kingdom, the primary goals of saving souls and strengthening the Church have always been lost. Only as today's Church leaders effectively use their spiritual weapons can they win in the tests of spiritual warfare.

Chapter 13

THE SELF-WILL TEST

Definition—When a leader realizes God is asking him to do something that counters his own plans or desires, the Self-will Test has begun. God has to break the self-will and personal ambition of every person He uses, so that He can trust him or her to do whatever He requires in His kingdom.

At times, He asks us to sacrifice even good and appropriate things. God will sometimes even request a man to do something for Him and give no logical reason for it. In not always explaining His request to leaders, God is developing a child-like faith and obedience in their hearts. This kind of simple faith is always very pleasing to the Lord. God will even ask His leaders to sacrifice to Him what they know to be God's will. In the case of Abraham, God asked him to sacrifice his son Isaac, God's promised seed (Genesis 22:1).

In all of this, a man's desires, thoughts, feelings and plans are put into subjection to God's will. This constant submission to the Lord's will is what true Christianity is all about. God does not necessarily prefer painful sacrifices from His leaders. But when he speaks something contrary to a man's desire, the man must quickly respond to the word.

Purpose–The Self-will Test subjects man's will to God's Word (both the written and quickened). In doing this, God helps us fulfill the scriptural admonition, "Let him who boasts, boast in the Lord (and not in man)" (I Corinthians 1:31). This is why God uses the foolish, despised, unexpected, and hateful things of this world for His kingdom, that He might receive all of the glory and credit for what is done (I Corinthians 1:26-31). Man's sinful nature pits his natural will against the spiritual will of God. God must therefore crucify a leader's desires, on occasion, so that He can accomplish His desires in His own way. Isaiah prophesied so appropriately:

ISAIAH 55:6-9

"Seek ye the Lord while he may be found, call ye upon him while he is near. Let the wicked forsake his way, and unrighteous man his thoughts; and let him return unto the Lord, and he will have mercy upon him; and to our God, for he will abundantly pardon. 'For my thoughts are not your thoughts, neither are your ways my ways,' saith the Lord.

'For as the heavens are higher than the earth, so are my ways higher than your ways, and my thoughts than your thoughts!'"

Biblical Illustration—the Lord Jesus Christ (Matthew 26): The very famous passage of Jesus' final submission to the heavenly Father's will, before He went to the cross, demonstrates this submission of His own personal self-will:

MATTHEW 26:36-48

Then cometh Jesus with them unto a place called Gethsemane, and saith unto the disciples, 'Sit ye here, while I go and pray yonder.' And he took with him Peter and the two sons of Zebedee, and began to be sorrowful and very heavy. Then saith he unto them, 'My soul is exceeding sorrowful, even unto death: tarry ye here, and watch with me.' And he went a little farther, and fell on his face, and prayed, saying, 'O my Father, if it be possible, let this cup pass from me: nevertheless not as I will, but as thou wilt.' And he cometh unto the disciples, and findeth them asleep, and saith unto Peter, 'What, could ye not watch with me one hour? Watch and pray, that ye enter not into temptation: the spirit indeed is willing, but the flesh is weak.' He went away again the second time, and prayed, saying, 'O my Father, if this cup may not pass away from me, except I drink it, thy will be done.' And he came and found them asleep again: for their eyes were heavy. And he left them, and went away again, and prayed the third time, saying the same words. Then cometh he to his disciples, and saith unto them, 'Sleep on now, and take your rest; behold, the hour is at hand, and the Son of man is betrayed into the hands of sinners. Rise, let us be going; behold, he is at hand that doth betray me.' And while he yet spake, lo, Judas, one of the twelve, came, and with him a great multitude with swords and staves, from the chief priests and elders of the people. Now he that betrayed him gave them a sign, saying, 'Whomsoever I shall kiss, that same is he: hold him fast.'"

Here we see that, in His human self, Jesus did not want to suffer the experience of the cross. His divine nature desired the cross as the will of the Father who sent Him, but it was not so with His human nature.

Every leader in God's kingdom must lay down his plans and desires to fulfill God's will, even as

Jesus did. Only as we lay down our fleshly and carnal ambitions can God use each of us as a vessel for His glory.

Chapter 14

THE VISION TEST

Definition–The Vision Test occurs when contrary people and circumstances besiege a leader's spiritual insight into the purposes of God. Natural and physical vision is not enough for a leader of God's people. He must also have spiritual eyes of faith to see God's will and desire for His people. The spiritual Vision Test asks two main questions: "Can you see the spiritual needs and answers of the people of God?" and, "Can you resist opposition and adversity, and tenaciously hold the vision that God has given you as a leader?"

Purpose—The Vision Test shows a leader how shallow his spiritual insight really is. Every leader feels he has a measure of insight into God and His people; otherwise he could not serve the Lord in a ministry capacity. All leaders are tempted to think that their present education, insight, knowledge, and wisdom is totally sufficient to meet the challenges of Church life. "After all," many exclaim, "wasn't I fully trained in the seminary or Bible college for this ministry?"

The plain answer is, "No!" No leader receives full training for the ministry in a seminary or a Bible college. God desires to keep His leaders constantly dependent on Him and His Spirit, and not dependent solely on their abilities, past training, or experience. At this point, unfortunately, many who are called to a ministry fail. When they begin to see what it actually takes to walk by faith and minister by the power of the Holy Spirit, they cannot bear being so humbled!

Many of their friends had told them, "Oh, you will make such a good minister. You will really be able to do a lot for God because you have so many talents and abilities!" The school textbooks told them, "Now this is the way to run a service, and this is the way to preach a sermon, and this is the way to save souls, and this is the way to cause the church to grow." But when those called of God graduate from formal education and get away from their friends, everything changes. They find that the true spiritual success of their ministries depends on different criteria than their friends or textbooks told them! What do they do then? They either drop in defeat or desperately call on God. Only the latter make it.

The Vision Test also ensures that the glory for success goes to God. A vision from the Lord may seem to die once, or even twice, so that its final fulfillment gives God much more glory than an uninterrupted march to success. God receives much glory when a vision is fulfilled supernaturally and in God's way.

Biblical Illustration—Nehemiah (Nehemiah 1,2,4): The story of Nehemiah's Vision Test, and its fulfillment, have two major elements. First, Nehemiah had spiritual eyes of faith to see the needs and answers of God's people in Jerusalem after the Babylonian captivity. Nehemiah describes the scene:

NEHEMIAH 1:1 – 2:6

"The words of Nehemiah, the son of Hachaliah. And it came to pass in the month Chisleu, in the twentieth year, as I was in Shushan the palace, that Hanani, one of my brethren, came, he and certain men of

Judah; and I asked them concerning the Jews that had escaped, which were left of the captivity, and concerning Jerusalem. And they said unto me, 'The remnant that are left of the captivity there in the province are in great affliction and reproach: the wall of Jerusalem also broken down, and the gates thereof are burned with fire.' And it came to pass, when I heard these words, that I sat down and wept, and mourned certain days and fasted and prayed before the God of heaven, and said, 'I beseech thee, O Lord God of heaven, the great and terrible God, that keepeth covenant and mercy for them that love him and observe his commandments; let thine ear now be attentive, and thine eyes open, that thou mayest hear the prayer of thy servant, which I pray before thee now, day and night, for the children of

Israel thy servants, and confess the sins of the children of Israel which we have sinned. We have dealt very corruptly against thee, and have not kept thy commandments, nor thy statutes, nor thy judgments, which thou commandedst thy servant Moses. Remember, I beseech thee, the word that thou commandedst thy servant Moses, saying, 'If ye transgress, I will scatter you abroad among the nations: but if you turn unto me, and keep my commandments, and do them; though there were of you cast out unto the uttermost part of the heaven, yet will I gather thee from thence, and will bring thee unto the place that I have chosen to set my name there! Now these are thy servants and thy people, whom thou hast redeemed by thy great power, and by thy strong hand. O Lord, I beseech thee, let now thine ear be attentive to the prayer of thy servant, and to the prayer of thy servants, who desire to fear thy name: and prosper, I pray thee, thy servant this day, and grant him mercy in the sight of this man.' For I was the king's cup-bearer. And it came to pass in the month Nisan, in the twentieth year of Artaxerxes, the king, that wine was before him: and I took up the wine, and gave it unto the king. Now I had not been beforetime sad in his presence. Wherefore, the king said unto me, 'Why is thy countenance sad, seeing thou art not sick? This is nothing else but sorrow of heart.' Then I was very sore afraid, and said unto the king, 'Let the king live forever: why should not my countenance be sad, when the city, the place of my fathers' sepulchres, lieth waste and the gates thereof are consumed with fire?' Then the king said unto me, 'For what dost thou make request?' So I prayed to the God of heaven. And I said unto the king, 'If it please the king, and if thy servant has found favour in thy sight, that thou wouldest send me unto Judah, unto the city of my fathers' sepulchres, that I may build it.' And the king said unto me, (the queen also sitting next to him) 'For how long shall thy journey be? And when wilt thou return?' So it pleased the king to send me; and I set him a time."

Nehemiah knew that the Jews could not serve the Lord without their city, walls, and temple being rebuilt. He desired God to use him to restore the ways that his people would use to worship God. He spiritually recognized that his people had sinned against God's law (Nehemiah 1:7-9) and had thus incurred God's judgment upon them.

This should be the spiritual vision of every true leader. Each must see where the Church has sinned against God, and then help to regain God's blessing through repentance, faith, and obedience to His Word. Secondly, Nehemiah's commitment to his spiritual vision from the Lord did not buckle under adverse circumstances. Note what this leader did in time of opposition:

NEHEMIAH 4:6-10

"So, built we the wall; and all the wall was joined together unto the half thereof; for the people had a mind to work. But it came to pass, that when Sanballat, and Tobiah, and the Arabians, and the Ammonites, and Ashdodites, heard that the walls of Jerusalem were made up, and that the breeches began to be stopped, then they were very wroth, and conspired all of them together to come and to fight against Jerusalem, and to hinder it. Nevertheless, we made our prayer unto our God, and set a watch against them day and night, because of them. And Judah said, 'The strength of the bearers of burdens is decayed, and there is much rubbish, so that we are not able to build the wall.'"

Nehemiah did not allow the enemies of Judah to discourage him in his vision. Instead, he gave himself to prayer. Similarly, every leader should never allow negative people or circumstances to cause him to lose the vision that God has given him for the Church.

Chapter 15

THE USAGE TEST

Definition—A leader undergoes the Usage Test in his life or ministry preparation when he cannot find the need, demand, opportunity, invitation, results, or expected occasion to exercise his ministry. "Put on the shelf" is a common description for this situation.

Purpose—God may put a leader "on the shelf" temporarily for several reasons.

First, God may desire to show the leader that he depends too heavily on his actual service or activity, rather than upon the Lord Himself, for his joy and spiritual fulfillment. Being "on the shelf" may stimulate the leader to develop his personal prayer and life in the Word far more than ministry success would.

God may desire to humble the leader. A leader who is greatly used of God may become proud and self-sufficient. He may need to lose part or all of his public ministry to see that his power and ability are not the true reasons for his accomplishments in the kingdom. God is more inclined to use a man's weakness for His glory than to use his strengths. It is simply human nature to credit men for being the source of their strengths, especially their obvious ones.

The Usage Test also gives God an opportunity to purify the motives of His leaders. What causes a leader to act or speak the way he does? Why does he do the things that he does? Many times a leader's motivation will turn from pure ministry service to building a personal kingdom. The name of Jesus Christ, saving souls, and edifying the Church may take the back seat to highlighting the leader's ministry and reputation. God must set this kind of leader on the shelf to purify His motives. Otherwise, this leader will take many into spiritual destruction with himself.

The Usage Test may also deepen the message of the leader. Many leaders live on their past sermons and messages without getting fresh words or experiences from God. Some leaders stay so busy that they either do not have, or do not take the time, to deepen their messages. But the flock of God cannot constantly feed from the same pasture of sermons without growing thin and hungry for more. God must sometimes put a minister out of public commission for awhile so that he will be motivated to deepen his understanding of the

Word of God. After a leader's messages deepen, he can return to give the sheep a much more enriching diet.

Biblical Illustration—John the Baptist (Matthew 3; Mark 1, Luke 1,3; John 1): John was born (c. 7 B.C.) to Zacharias and Elizabeth, and was raised and called to the prophetic ministry in the wilderness of Judea (Luke 1:80 and 3:2). He was the forerunner of the Messiah, and the last and greatest member of the prophetic guild before the kingdom of God was proclaimed. For a man whom Jesus Himself highly honored, he had a very humble attitude. But he had a rather brief period of ministry.

John's humble attitude is shown by the words which he said to Christ when the Messiah came to him for baptism: "I have need to be baptized by You, and do You come to me?" (Matthew 3:14). His lowly attitude also appears when he preached about Christ, "After me comes one who is mightier than I, and I am not even fit to stoop down and untie the thongs of his sandals" (Mark 1:7). John recognized that although he held an important place in God's economy, it was his purpose to lead men to Jesus Christ, even his own disciples (John 1:35-37). Every leader in the Church must know that the entire purpose of his service to God is in leading men to know and to serve the Savior.

John was also willing to accept a longer time of preparation than his actual period of ministry. Luke 1:80 states, "And the child (John) continued to grow, and to become strong in spirit, and he lived in the deserts until the day of his public appearance to Israel." This preparation time in the desert was probably much longer than the duration of his active ministry. This is a definite part of the Usage Test. Sometimes a leader's service is so unique in kind or timing that God extends his preparation for reasons known only to Himself.

How many leaders would complain if they had to spend thirty years in preparation for a three and a half year ministry, as our Lord did? Most leaders are so service-minded that they think they would be doing their best for God if they spent only three and a half years in preparation for a thirty year ministry! Every leader, however, must accept God's full time of preparation for his ministry. The length of preparation differs for every leader. It will depend on God's call on his life, his cooperation with the dealings of God, and the future extent of his ministry. God must be trusted wholeheartedly in the fulfillment of all of the details of a leader's ministry, including the timing.

John the Baptist also was willing to be used of God only as long as God sovereignly intended to use him. John condemned Herod the tetrarch for many evil things, including marriage to Herodias, his brother's wife. For this, Herod had John imprisoned and beheaded. What an inglorious death for one of the greatest eschatalogical prophets of all time—a short ministry, ending in decapitation! John was totally submitted to the will of God and God's Usage Test. He did not complain in prison about "being on the shelf," but submitted to God's timing for the end of his ministry.

In the same way, every leader should have a light "grip" on his gift and ministry. He or she must allow God to remove these at any time without complaining, doubting, or grumbling. May every leader submit all of the aspects of his ministry to God, especially its timing and usage, throughout all its stages. May all leaders keep their hearts so humble and dependent upon the Lord that He may approve their total patience and trust in Him, even through the Usage Test.

AFTERWORD

The tests described in this book may come especially during the early stages of a leader's ministry. But they can come at any time—as they did for the men we used for biblical illustrations. Governmental ministries face what may be a "hotter" refiner's fire, yet God takes all Christians through these tests to refine their faith. Because God's imagination is limitless, so are His ways of bringing His children to maturity. This book has described only the more common tests that appear throughout Scripture.

As we have seen, the Bible is full of examples of

God testing His leaders. From the frequency of such instances, God appears to be a God of testing. Hebrews 12:29 states, "For our God is a consuming fire." As a consuming and testing fire, God tries the attitudes and motives of each of the people He uses. This is not simply to expose weaknesses, but to cause them to turn to the Lord for help. God proves His vessels of leadership, already knowing their inner weaknesses, that these might be healed.

From the previous examples, we've also seen that God will test and try a leader to purify him. Through trials and tough circumstances, God removes attitudes of bitterness, selfishness, and covetousness from a leader's heart, and replaces them with motives of love.

Another purpose in God's testing that has been illustrated in this book is to sort out those who are not truly called by Him. As we've seen, God puts His leaders in desperate situations. Those who do not feel a true call of the Spirit upon their lives drop out of the preparation process.

A final reason that God tests His leaders is to equip them with the spiritual understanding they need to help His people. All Christians experience a variety of tests and trials. Only the leader who has successfully overcome them himself can help the people.

Be encouraged! Though the tests that God gives may be painful, men and women who can keep believing and trusting in the living God during problems and difficulties will develop true faithfulness to God and His Word. Take comfort in knowing that God is using these tests to build and grow you, not to tear you down.

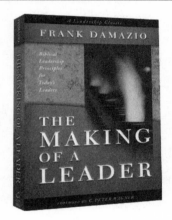

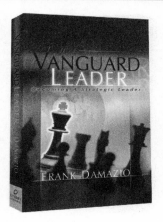

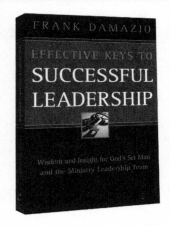

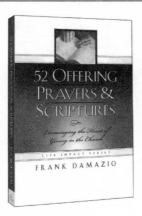